WHAT THEY WANT US TO KNOW

Shawndra McWhorter

WHAT THEY WANT US TO KNOW

Cover Design & Interior Format by The Killion Group, Inc.

TABLE OF CONTENTS

ACKNOWLEDGMENTS

First and foremost, my deepest love and gratitude to my mother, my father, and my sister. They have loved and accepted me just as I am, all my life. Even when it wasn't convenient, easy, or making sense.

To the teachers and healers in my life: Dr. Jeri Ryan, Sarah Negus (The Modern Day Shaman®), Cary Hamilton, LMHC, Lynne McTaggart, and my Power of Eight group (Devi, Gilliane, Jeni, John, Laurel, Michelle, Nancy, Sally, Tim and Tina), and John Utter (Thrive at Work.

To Karen Roy, Book Coach Bookcoachingacademy. com, for her invaluable assistance as my writing coach.

To my amazing friends who have supported and loved me no matter what—Susan, Crissy, Michele, Kelly, and Brian.

To Carrie, Natalie, Deanna, Hayley and everyone at The Unapologetic Voice House. You have all been brilliant and amazing to work with.

Last, and certainly not least, the animals that have shared my path and taught me more about unconditional love, devotion, determination, and how to be the best human I can be: Ringo, Sparky, King Elvis, Miss Scooby Doo, Ralph, Chico, June Bug, Oso, Nikki, Samson, Moose, Joshua, Akela, Joey, Cochise, Casper, Stone, and Norman.

DEDICATION

This book is dedicated to every animal I've encountered who has taught me how to be a more compassionate, tolerant, understanding, and grateful human being.

My goal is to be the kind of human they believe me to be.

INTRODUCTION

M Y CONNECTION TO ANIMALS GOES back to my earliest memories growing up in Southern California. As a toddler, I can remember moving snails out of the way so they wouldn't get stepped on. I couldn't bear the thought of them being killed when all I had to do was help them get out of the way. I remember wondering why other people didn't do the same thing. Adults must have thought I was crazy as I picked them up, gently put them down—always in the direction they had been heading!—and told them to be safe. Even back then I was talking to animals. I was amazed by the snails and would gently touch their antennae, watching in fascination as each antenna would go down and come back up again.

When I was about four or five years old, I remember catching lizards with my bare hands and being enthralled at how their little feet felt in my hands. I'd gently hold them for a bit and then let them be on their way. It only took me one time, though, to learn something crucial about their tails . . . They would come off when distressed! I remember being horrified that I had wounded or killed one when I grabbed it by the tail and the tail came off in my hand! My mother had to keep reassuring me that it would grow back, that I hadn't destroyed the lizard. The experience, however, taught me that there are consequences to my actions, and I simply needed to be more careful.

I look back now and am amazed that I was even able

to catch them. Or did they *let* me catch them?

I clearly remember the last one I ever caught. I was seven years old and came upon a gorgeous, large lizard. I was so excited to hold it and see it up close. Well, it turned out the lizard hadn't wanted that at all and chomped down on my finger! Then I realized that I had picked up an alligator lizard. These are larger lizards with fairly big teeth, and he was not happy that I had invaded his space. And even though he didn't want to be held, he wasn't letting go of my finger! My parents and I still laugh about how I ran across the yard screaming to my father to make this lizard let go of me. Eventually, my father was able to pry the lizard's teeth off my finger and let him go. Part of me had been scared of the blood and the pain, but there had also been a part of me that was so sad. It kind of broke my little heart that he didn't want to play with me, and I never tried to catch another lizard after that.

I grew up northeast of San Diego, California, where there's desertlike terrain with lots of fruit trees and dusty trails to explore, along which were things that could kill us or make us very ill. Things like rattlesnakes, black widow spiders, scorpions, and tarantulas. My sister and I were taught early on to be aware of their presence and to pay close attention to where they might be. We were also taught that if we didn't bother them, they usually wouldn't bother us, and we did find that to be true. I was cautious of these creatures, but I still found beauty in each, even if I wasn't interested in holding them. That alligator lizard had taught me that valuable lesson!

When I was in high school, my family watched a documentary about a man who would do "thought commands" with his border collie. Basically, he would read a card with a command on it, look at the dog, think the command over and over, and then the dog would do what the man was thinking. We tried it with our border collie, Oso, and we could see that she understood us and would do what we "asked" of her—when she felt like it. Then there were times when she would just turn her back, lie down, and ignore us. We knew she understood us; she just didn't care what we wanted her to do. It didn't occur to me then that Oso was also communicating; I just wasn't listening.

In 2000, I rescued a dog named Joey who had been severely abused by his owner. A family friend's elderly neighbor had passed away and left his dog behind, and our friend had asked if I would be able to take him or foster him. She brought Joey over that evening for us to meet, and I knew right away that he would be staying with me. There was something about how he and I connected that I couldn't put into words. Plus, I knew that older dogs don't get adopted from shelters the way puppies do, and I could not bear the thought of Joey being locked in a crate all alone. It just wasn't an option for me to consider; he was to be a member of my family.

Joey was a ninety-pound black Labrador retriever, and he was about five years old when I adopted him. I didn't know anything about the abuse at that point. He was just a big, happy dog, and he was thrilled to play and be loved. I learned later on that he was also grateful to be safe for the first time in his life. The years of abuse, though, had made him dangerous. Joey had nearly attacked me several times and did end up attacking my father. I was desperate for answers and a way to help him, so I found Dr. Jeri Ryan, an animal communicator out of the Oakland area.

At the time, I hadn't even known such people existed, but I knew without a doubt that it was real. Dr. Ryan was a child psychologist, specializing in childhood trauma, and she used her extensive training and knowledge to help animals, as well. Joey ended up being euthanized—more about that later in the book—but that one dog and that one animal communicator started me on a path of love, awareness, connection, and healing that I will forever be grateful for. It also just so happened that Dr. Ryan was teaching a class in my area a few months later, and of course, I signed up.

Joey changed my life in a way that nothing and no one else has. This one, beautiful, amazing, tortured soul opened my eyes to a path I didn't know existed but one that I was destined to travel. I've tried to locate Dr. Ryan since then without success, but I'd love for her to know what she helped bring about and how grateful I am for what she shared with me.

This book is the culmination of a lifetime connection to animals and to that *knowing* I've always had that animals have something important to share with us. All my life, I've felt more comfortable with animals than with most humans. It's not that I dislike humans at all, but animals aren't intentionally cruel, they've never laughed at my pain or my missteps, they are exactly who they are without apology or compromise—wild or domestic— and I love that about them. I've always thought that if humans would be more like animals, we'd have a much kinder and happier world.

The knowings that I have are what guide me, and have always guided me, whether it was to deploy to Louisiana after Hurricane Katrina and help rescue animals, to stand up for those not able to speak for themselves, or to defend the rights of others even when the majority doesn't. These knowings have never failed me. Even during times when I was afraid others would think I was crazy by talking with animals, I still did it. In the beginning, I was very cautious about who I would share my animal communication skills with. I'm not sure if I just didn't want to get into an argument about it or if I just wasn't confident enough in my skills yet, but either way, it was not something that I openly broadcasted for quite some time.

Since about 2004, I've known that I would write this book. I knew the title, and I knew the concept. What I didn't know, though, was that it would take until 2020 to be written. My intent with this book is to honor these knowings and share the translated messages from some of the animals I've come in contact with. And for anyone who is ready to listen with their heart, to find the unity and connection in all living beings, I hope you come back to the photos again and again to hear the specific messages they have for *you*. Ever since I was a little girl, I've known I was here to leave this world more balanced than I found it. This book is one step toward that.

CHAPTER ONE

ANIMAL COMMUNICATION

IF YOU'RE NEW TO ANIMAL communication, you may be wondering if it's real. It is. It's also something that any of us can do. It takes training and practice, but it's most definitely real and possible. I'll bet most of us have been talking to our pets for years, not really thinking of it as communication. The main difference with what I'm referring to as animal communication is the listening part. We've probably all heard the saying about having two ears and one mouth: listen more and talk less! That's the perfect motto for animal communication. There's also the saying about the longest journey we'll travel is the twelve inches from our head to our hearts. Animal communication is about tuning into your heart and listening with your soul. Your brain is still active, of course, but your heart is now leading the way.

A friend referred a woman named Melissa to me for some help with her horse, Jazz. I had never met Melissa or Jazz. I never had the opportunity to even pet Jazz. But Jazz came into my life and proved to me that I wasn't making up stories, that I was being told things I couldn't know unless I was actually communicating with the animal. Jazz was strong, gorgeous, and full of personality. He lived with his human family, a mule, goats, and several cows. Jazz had displacement colic, in which a horse's small intestine becomes twisted and can cause the large intestine to become displaced and restrict blood flow. This type of colic requires immediate surgery, or it can be life-threatening. Unfortunately, Jazz didn't live long enough to make it to surgery.

Jazz had lived with three humans in his life, the first being a woman who loved him but moved across the country and had to give him up. The second human was a man who then sold Jazz to the third and final person in his life, Melissa. The very day after Jazz had died, Melissa reached out and asked me to talk with him. Yes, even after death, we can communicate; animals proved to me that the body may die, but the spirit does not. Melissa and I spoke for thirty minutes or so in order for me to get to know her and Jazz. After we hung up, I quieted myself, and I tuned in to Jazz and shared what Melissa wanted me to say: *I love you. I'm sorry. I did everything I could. Are you okay?* All the things that most of us would want to say to an animal we lost.

At the very beginning, Jazz showed me an image of him and a woman inside a barn, his right front hoof in a bucket. It was a calm, reassuring feeling. Throughout the conversation, I kept seeing a humanlike smile in my mind's eye, so I would write it down every time he shared it. I shared with him all that Melissa wanted me to share, and at the end, I asked Jazz if he had anything he'd like to say or share.

He said, "Tell her to plant the flowers I love." Jazz then showed me what those flowers looked like. I didn't know what they were but I wrote down the best description of them I could.

I typed up the conversation and e-mailed it to Melissa. She called me back, very excited. Melissa then explained how when she first brought Jazz home, he had a large abscess on his right front hoof, and twice a day for almost a week, she and Jazz would stand inside the barn while he soaked his hoof in a bucket.

My first thought was, *There's no way I could have guessed that!*

Melissa and I talked about the smile that Jazz had

showed me, and it didn't really feel like it made sense so we let it go. The flowers, though! She told me that one day Jazz had gotten out of his pasture and made his way to the flowers she had planted along the side of her house, and he ate every one of them!

"You know what kind of flowers they are, right?" she asked me.

I didn't, so she excitedly told me, "Forget-me-nots."

I was completely stunned. If I was this blown away by one conversation, how much more was I in store for?

Almost a year later, Melissa called me again. She had been contacted by Jazz's first person—the woman who moved across the country. This woman was back on the West Coast for a bit, tracked down Melissa, and called to see if she could come visit Jazz. Unfortunately, Melissa had to tell her that Jazz had not survived colic.

She was so sorry to hear that, of course, but then she said, "You know, I always thought that if he could, he would have had a smile on his face all the time."

What? Jazz had shared a message for a woman that we had never met and had no intention of ever coming into contact with.

This further proved to me that animal communication is real. There is so much more going on and accessible to us—a lot we just don't fully understand. Not understanding it, though, doesn't prevent it from being real. This one conversation made me think about all the messages I may have missed or hadn't paid attention to. And it made me want to be much more attentive to what was happening around me. What were the possibilities available to us? What if more humans listened? How many more humans and animals could be helped?

This book is meant to help us listen, to have deeper connections, and to sit with these shared messages to see how they might impact our own lives. Animals invite each of us to explore deeper, to expand our beliefs, to consider new paths in our lives. We all have free will, so we get to choose what feels right to us and to our lives in any given moment. These messages from animals are sent without judgment or shame, and I encourage you to accept them with that intent.

When you look at the picture of each animal I share with you, do so with an open mind. Let go of any assumptions or guesses prior to reading what they have to say. Many times, we're very quick to use our ability to read someone. While that can be a useful skill to have in our day-to-day lives, in these instances, it may not be the case. For example, I rescued a dog named Cochise who always looked very serious in his photos. Cochise was a medium-sized mixed-breed dog who had the softest ears you've ever felt. I used to tell him all the time how much I loved him and his velvety ears. But because he looked so serious, there were people who would immediately think he was sad, or abused, or lonely. He was none of those things! He was a happy, healthy, spoiled, deeply loved dog who just didn't look the way we think a happy dog *should.*

Take a look at the photo of him below, and you'll see what I mean. I wonder sometimes if he wanted to send a deeper message to those who saw his picture. Could he have been offering them a way to look inside and question their preconceived notions about what "happy" looks like? I think he was.

Cochise and his seriousness.

As you read the animals' messages in the following several chapters, you will notice some interjections from me in brackets. I do this to bring clarification, context, more detail, feelings, actions, and so forth, but please note that the text within those brackets were not their actual words. The process as I communicated with each of the animals in this book ended up being quite different from conversations I've had in the past. Normally, a human reaches out to me with a request or an issue to discuss—anything from helping a dog understand the process of flying to questions about how an animal feels about cancer treatments. In these instances, it's normally a back-and-forth conversation, and I'm connected more with their physical selves. We're addressing their likes and dislikes, their needs, their preferences, et cetera. The messages in this book, however, were really them talking and me transcribing. My process was to quiet my mind, ground myself, tune in to each animal, and then introduce myself and explain what I was doing. Actually, I didn't have to do much explaining at all. They seemed to already know what I was looking for. It was more of a "download" from them than anything.

For these conversations, I was connected to their higher selves, not the physical, as well. So it wasn't about what their bodies wanted or needed but what their souls wanted us to know and understand. It was also less about their individual personalities and focused on a much deeper connection with us all. Once the animals in this book started talking, I was just writing down everything they said verbatim. So if you see questions, it's the animal asking the questions. And yes, it was done using pen and paper. It may take longer, but doing so seems to provide a deeper connection than typing on a computer or making an audio recording. But that's just what feels right for me.

As I was writing their words, it was very clear to me what their tones and feelings were. I hope you are able to pick up their tone, as well, from the nurturing calmness of Princess Angeline to the forthright, rather firm tone of Cougar and everything in between. Their stories are not my words. I'm merely giving voice to what they have to say. In every case, though, the animals speak with respect, kindness, and a complete lack of blame or shame. They fully understand that we get to choose our own paths, and they have a strong desire to help us walk a kinder and more compassionate path, one that is more deeply connected to them and to Source. When I say 'Source', I'm referring to a higher power – whether it be God, Goddess, Allah, Buddha, Spirit, The Great Unknown, Grandfather – whatever name you give to that which has given us life, is what I mean by 'Source'.

Other than correcting spelling and punctuation, and making some small grammar tweaks, what you'll read is what they said to me exactly. None of the meaning and true content has been altered. I asked them what they wanted us to know, and they shared from their souls. They are opening doors and giving us tools to navigate our way on these new paths. We each get to choose whether we walk through those doors or not. At the end of each conversation, I've added my impressions to provide a little more clarity to what they've shared. I've also included some suggestions and considerations as to how you can open your heart and walk through these doors they've opened to find more meaning and balance in your life and in our world.

I finally began writing this book during the COVID-19 pandemic, while most of us were in lockdown. Also during this time, we were hearing loud, clear voices to bring about the end of systemic racism in our culture— mainly in the United States but supported all over—the racial injustices, inequalities, assaults, and murders. We seem to be going through a much-needed global shift, and I believe the animals will assist us in this transition. I didn't know who would show up to share, nor did I know what they would be sharing. I believe, though, that their insights can be of service to any of us who are ready to find a more balanced and tolerant way of living.

This book is meant to be read in any way that resonates with you. You can read start to finish. You can start at the back. You can scan the Table of Contents to see which animal calls to you. You can flip through the pages until you feel compelled to stop. Whatever feels right for you *is* right! As you begin your journey reading these conversations, however you choose to do so, I hope you find some of what you are seeking and a deeper meaning in the connection. May this journey expand your idea of what is possible, what is real, and what matters. Listen with your heart, and welcome any messages they have for you in addition to what's in this book. The blank pages in the back are for you to write down any extra information they may share with you. Be open to words, feelings, images, visions, or just knowings. I'm excited for you to read their messages, and I'm excited for them to finally be heard.

CHAPTER TWO

PALAU JELLYFISH

IN 2011, I WAS FORTUNATE enough to travel to Koror, Palau. Palau is a gorgeous and amazing country in the western Pacific Ocean, about a thousand miles east of the Philippines. On one island in Palau, Eil Malk, is known for an amazing marine lake called Jellyfish Lake. This lake houses millions of fairly small jellyfish that you can snorkel with. Really! You can swim among them, something I would never knowingly do with the jellyfish in Southern California.

Jellyfish Lake is connected to the ocean through fissures and tunnels in the limestone and is incredibly unique. The golden jellyfish (Mastigias cf. papua etpisoni) that populate the lake can and do sting, but they normally don't sting humans—we're not a food source for them as they mainly feed on algae. I was told that no one is allowed to dive too deep as the water becomes toxic, and that there were crocodiles in the area. But I wanted to swim with the jellyfish so bad, I didn't care about any of it. I didn't see a crocodile the entire time I was in Palau, let alone one in Jellyfish Lake.

When I was in the water with the jellyfish, they swam so close that I could touch them, some even bumping up against me. I almost can't describe the feeling. They were so smooth and soft, so gentle around me—and there were so many of them! Swimming with them was one of the most incredible experiences of my life, and I honestly did not want to leave. In fact, at one point,

I looked up from the water and could see the people I'd come with sitting on the dock waiting for me. I knew I had to go back, and it made me a little sad. So I started slowly swimming back to the dock. It seemed to be taking forever, though, so I looked up again. I had somehow done a one-eighty and was heading the wrong way! I just laughed at myself and started really heading back this time.

The picture below is a screen capture from my underwater video camera, and the little dots you see in the picture are actually jellyfish. It's funny, too, because I thought my camera was only recording the images, but it turns out it also recorded the audio. When I played it back, I could hear myself laughing and squealing with excitement through my snorkel. It was so much fun I want to go back again!

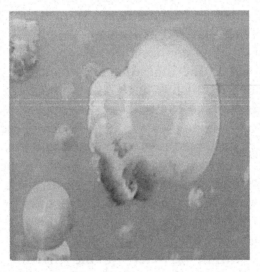

MESSAGE FROM THE JELLYFISH

Hello, Travelers. Hello, Seekers. We applaud you for making this journey. We all hope to share many truths with you and open your hearts to something new, something you might have thought you didn't know, or even believe, but something that reaches your soul and helps you remember what you've always known. We are all connected. What one does to another impacts [us] all. Not only in the physical sense but also in the spiritual and etheric sense. Each time you speak a kind word or make a choice to not judge another, you are creating ripples and waves that resonate with a frequency of love and gratitude.

We, the jellyfish, are highly attuned in our physical bodies to perceive these frequencies. We are also highly attuned on an energetic level. We need both, just as all life on Earth does. We are all our physical selves just as much as we are our energetic selves. It seems as if many humans are more in tune with their physical selves, but they also seek to find or reconnect to their energetic selves. Both are always there for you. Always.

Where do you focus? Do you perceive a lack of your energetic self? There is no lack. There is just more focus on the physical. Shift with the tides of energy. Be like a jellyfish and gently find your way. Find your rhythm [with] each [part of yourself], knowing they are both always with you. You cannot have one without the other—unless, of course, you are no longer residing in your physical self.

So, if we always have both, why do some [beings] perceive to have only one, or both but not in balance? This is why you're here, Seekers and Travelers. To open your hearts to remembering that you are both. You have always been both, and the balance you seek is already there for you. Notice what you focus on. How much of what you call "time," do you spend on your energetic self each day? Just because you do not focus on it doesn't mean it isn't there. It's always there.

Humans—those of you who are connecting with us—feel the love we are sending you right now. Yes. Stop and feel us sending you love. [They pause.]

Feel yourself among us, floating gently and being

surrounded with love and acceptance. We love you. We love your path. We love all of you. We are love, and we invite you to be love, too. During times of fear or distress, tune in to the feeling you just experienced and pull it to you. Let us assist you in maintaining your flow with *all* that is.

INSIGHTS

The feeling of ease with this communication is amazing. The jellyfish are beginning this journey for us with so much love, acceptance, and grace. Their desire for each of us to feel this safety and comfort is palpable and unconditional. It reminds me of what I felt when I was in the water with them—such incredible calmness and connection. I invite you to take the jellyfish up on their offer of tuning in to them and feel them sending you love.

CONSIDERATIONS

Take a few moments to slow down and focus on the jellyfish. You can look at the picture if it helps you. Notice your inhale and your exhale. Visualize them swimming with that same rhythm. Let yourself notice what you feel without analyzing it, questioning it, or judging it. If you hear yourself using phrases like "I should have," "Why didn't I," "I never seem to," et cetera, just recognize that these could be shaming or blaming phrases that are not very helpful, and they are probably things you'd never say to another person. Just let those phrases pass you by and welcome in much more compassionate and tolerant thoughts.

Once you've experienced that feeling and your connection is strong with the jellyfish, take it a step further and send them your love. It can be something as simple as sending a beam of white or golden light directly from your heart to them. As you exhale, visualize that light and your love reaching the jellyfish. Just trust and send them love.

After you've received and sent them love, open your heart to what the jellyfish may have to share with you. Notice your feelings, any images you see, and feel how they feel about you. Again, do so without judgment or analysis. Trust that they love you and will share an image of yourself that you're ready to see, knowing that it will be beautiful, kind, and loving.

CHAPTER THREE

JAZZ THE HORSE

AS I MENTIONED IN CHAPTER one, Jazz was a horse who died of colic. I never met him in person, but I spoke with him the day after he passed away. I'm not sure what breed of horse he was or even how old he was. I do know, though, that he was far more connected to his higher self and a Higher Power than I could have imagined. Jazz was the first animal I had spoken to who had passed away, and he made it abundantly clear that he was still with us and wanted to engage in the conversation. I remember seeing that smile he kept sending and writing it down every time.

I'm so glad I learned not to question anything that the animals share with me. It's not my place to make sense of what they send, or even decide what is important or not. It's up to me to trust the connection and honor what they say or share by passing it on in as raw a form as possible. What someone else does with the message is entirely up to that person.

The one conversation I had with Jazz changed my entire perspective on how I thought things worked in the world. He turned it completely inside out and helped me look at things with a much more open heart and open mind. Even as I just wrote that, I thought to myself, *One conversation? Why didn't I ever go back again?*

I don't have a good answer to that, except maybe I wasn't ready to hear more. Maybe my soul knew to just integrate what he had shared and move forward with it.

So I'm here with him now, asking for more and ready to listen.

MESSAGE FROM JAZZ

Hello. She planted the flowers I love, didn't she? [He smiles.] She also passed along my message to my first person, didn't she? [He smiles again.] It brings me joy to know my messages were received! We are almost always sending messages out, and our souls sing whenever we know you hear them. There must be a purpose to all this, right? Many of us have asked ourselves that question, even those of us non-humans that are more deeply connected [to the higher realms] than some humans. There are times when we wonder what this is all about, especially when we see our humans hurting. It's at these times that the others [animals that have passed on, and Enlightened Beings] come and remind us of our purpose.

Our purpose is to feel, to question, to learn, to grow, to never stop moving. We see how some humans work very hard *not* to feel, *not* to question, *not* to go too deep. And that is the exact opposite of why we're here. We are all here to transcend our physical bodies while still in them! There doesn't have to be a physical death in order to transcend. Can you believe that? Does it seem possible? It is!

I can imagine many people were expecting [our] purpose to be something much deeper, more complicated, more difficult. And yet, as simple as [it] sounds, it actually may be one of the most difficult things that you ever do. How difficult could it be? It means feeling the Earth beneath your feet and all the life that courses through it. It means feeling the wind and understanding the power it carries. It means feeling [a] connection to every living thing. It doesn't mean just feeling happy or hopeful. It means feeling the fear of a trapped animal. It means feeling the hopelessness of a research animal. It also means feeling without judgment, without analyzing it, without fear or shame or blame or guilt. And that's where the difficulty comes in—asking your ego to set aside what it wants, what it thinks it should be doing, what it thinks should be happening, and just [feel]. And with that feeling comes an obligation to perhaps change how we do things, to take responsibility for what you can. I could see why people don't want to feel—not only because of the difficulty of setting aside your emotions and your grief and your sorrow at the things you can't change but also the responsibility for the things that you can change and don't. And yet there are those humans who do feel, who do wake up from their sleepwalking state, and not only see what's going on but allow themselves to *feel* what's going on. And with that feeling, with that knowledge, they take steps toward bringing balance [in our lives and in our world].

Oftentimes, these people are characterized as crazy or ridiculous or irrelevant in some way, but it's just because they are seeing and feeling with their hearts, with their souls, and they are exposing the fact that so many others are not. And it's so much easier to blame the crazy person or ridicule the irrelevant one. That's how you continue to hide. That's how you continue to pretend that you feel when you know in your heart that you do not.

This, too, could be the source of some of your struggle in life. So much of you *wants to* feel, *wants* to know, but there's also a part of you that just can't or won't allow that to happen. I believe that's one reason you could be here right now: to find the safety, the courage, the strength in numbers to let that part of your soul open up and *feel*.

Feel the emotions more than you have before—all of them—and know that it will not break you. Know that by feeling and acknowledging whatever you feel, you can now address it, talk to it, understand it, and come to know it. Once you give yourself the freedom to know yourself more deeply, you can move forward in a more connected, open, aware, and genuine way.

None of this is meant to cause harm. That is not the goal! This is meant to heal, to evolve, to learn, and to awaken. Even if you're not ready right now, it's okay! You might be later. There is no one keeping score or tracking the speed of your journey. It's your journey to honor. Yes, we're connected, so does one journey affect another? Yes. Without judgment, though! That could be a new concept for some. Living this life without shame or judgment. Of course, we all want for each of you to travel the kindest path possible. *When* you get there, though, does not matter. We rejoice with you and for you throughout it all.

INSIGHTS

"We see how some humans work very hard not to feel, not to question, not to go too deep. And that is the exact opposite of why we're here."

This sentence for me was profound. There have been

many times in my life when I blocked my feelings because they felt far too painful or scary. The way that Jazz shares it, though, takes away some of that fear and also helps me understand *why* I should be open to actually feeling those things. If I allow myself to trust, to let go of the fear and really *feel*, what will happen? The logical part of my brain says that I'd recover more quickly if I didn't hold on to any emotions that are not serving my highest well-being. The emotional part of my brain tells me that I may even find the courage to go deeper and deeper, to ask myself questions that could lead to answers that will help me evolve into a more loving human. If I'm exposing my authentic self, then aren't I able to see and heal those parts of me that are ready to be healed?

"We are all here to transcend our physical bodies while still in them! There doesn't have to be a physical death in order to transcend. Can you believe that? Does it seem possible? It is!"

What?! Is this possible for us *regular* people, though? I can easily believe this statement for Nelson Mandela, Mother Teresa, the Dalai Lama, Desmond Tutu, and *those* kinds of people, but for you and me? I wasn't aware that this was an option for us. But when I open myself to acknowledging how that makes me feel, it resonates with me, and I can be open to the possibility of it being real for any of us. Once again, Jazz just blew me away, and I love it.

CONSIDERATIONS

Find one thing that you've stopped yourself from feeling because of fear or shame. Breathe into it, sit with it, and give yourself the freedom to feel a little bit of it. Not so much that you cause any harm, of course, but just a little to see if you can begin to address it, name it, et cetera, as Jazz suggests.

To go a bit deeper, begin to journal every day. My friend and mentor, Sarah Negus (The Modern Day Shaman®), teaches that journaling three pages every morning can be very healing, and I agree. I've used this process often, to let my mind just *go* and to release all that it's ready to release. This is done without any blame or shame. You get to write whatever you want or need to, and no one—including yourself—will be judging you. You may even get to the point where you can "free write," when you're not thinking about the words at all. They just pour out of you effortlessly.

Once you find that one—or more—thing in your life that you're ready to address or bring balance to, ask yourself if there's someone you trust to talk it over with. Saying something scary out loud in a safe place can be incredibly freeing and healing. Talk with your doctor, your mental health professional, a clergy member—anyone who is trained to listen and assist. If it's someone other than a professional, I'd suggest being very open about needing them to listen without judgment or blame—only listen. The goal is not for them to advise you or try to solve anything, just to listen with an open mind and let you explore your own thoughts and feelings more deeply in a safe way.

CHAPTER FOUR

TARANTULA

GROWING UP IN AN AREA with wild tarantulas, I learned to look for them and expect them just about anywhere. I remember the first time I saw one run, how absolutely amazed I was how fast it moved. I had been watering the plants and disturbed one, so it ran up the side of the house and then along the length of it. I just stood there in awe. I was also extremely grateful that it wasn't running *toward* me!

Even though the tarantulas I grew up around weren't deadly, they were still so large and impressive— definitely not something that I'd want jumping on me. I've had dreams about tarantulas dropping on my head and I wasn't concerned at all, but those were merely dreams. I admire tarantulas, their role in our ecosystems, and also their role in our spiritual growth; I just will admire them from a distance. My father has held a tarantula, let it crawl on his arm, and it was as docile as he'd been told it would be. I'll pass on that, though, and be happy to have a conversation with a tarantula instead.

MESSAGE FROM TARANTULA

Humans have placed great importance on feeding the ego and making it happy. Yet, no matter how much money, success, accumulation, or being "more than" [they are], it has not satisfied [them]. [They] still see and experience struggle, sadness, frustration, and emptiness, despite all that they have attained and fought so hard for. There are some humans who will stop at nothing to fill that void. They attempt to fill it with material things, harming others, killing others, torturing others— torturing themselves, even. And yet, the void remains unfilled.

At what point will humans realize that this path will never fill the void? Will humans only realize this after all has been destroyed? How far are humans willing to go, attempting to fill this void by any means other than the one that will [actually] fill it? You know what is meant by this—you know, your soul knows. Listen to it! Ask your ego to step back some and allow your soul to speak. What does it say? We all know that, in many cases, it will [say something] very different from what the ego has been saying. Are you able to sit in silence and listen without distraction? And by distraction, I mean TV's, phones, meaningless conversations—anything that pulls you away from the quiet of your true self. Are you able to find comfort and safety in [having] less than what someone else has? If you are willing to condone and support those who torture others (i.e., research animals, lab animals, animals for entertainment, et cetera), would you be willing to try the opposite?

What if I told you that what you seek is actually available to you? But not with currency, not with anger, not with force, not with anything that causes harm— but with love. Are you willing and able to let go of the search to satisfy the ego, which can never be satisfied fully, and begin a new search? One that satisfies your soul? One that helps another? One that values another no matter how different [they are from you]? One that finds beauty in balance for all?

How do you feel just reading these words? Do you feel calm and [resonant]? Or [do you feel] fear and disbelief? Neither is right; neither is wrong. Ask yourself why. Why do you feel what you feel? What is your body and your soul telling you with that feeling? Will you run from the answer or to that answer? Only you can answer that and only you know why. And only you can travel the next steps. Know and believe, though, [that] you are not alone on this path. You're not, you never have been, and you never will be.

[Tarantula smiles and connects back into Mother Earth.]

Insights

Tuning into Tarantula was a powerful experience for me. She opens up the conversation to why humans are the way they are. I see some of the people that never seem to have enough—whether it's material things, power, money, status, or something else—and I wonder at what point it will be enough for them. Will they ever be satisfied with what they've accumulated or accomplished?

The void she speaks of makes me realize that most of us truly do have our own void that we're trying to fill. What am I filling mine with? How am I helping—or not helping—others to fill their voids? At what point do we let go of the need to fill a void? Her words make me think that by seeing our own void for what it's showing us, we can finally let it go. If we're shifting our focus to what satisfies the soul, then we will no longer need to fill a void. And if we no longer have a never-ending void to fill, we can begin to see ourselves and others with more tolerance, love, and respect.

Oh, Tarantula, you are opening my heart more and more with every word.

CONSIDERATIONS

Start by looking at an area of your life with which you never seem to be satisfied. Is there a part of you that never seems to heal? Do you seem to be repeating lessons, or are you drawn to similar people and situations again and again? Is that your void? Are you filling it with the same actions or words again and again? See if you can name your void and what you're attempting to fill it with. Do your best to be kind to yourself and just name it without any emotions attached.

Now that you've named your void, shift your focus to your soul and ask what it is seeking and how you are helping to address that desire. Your ego may really try to block your soul from speaking here. If that happens, just gently and kindly ask your ego to let your soul speak. You're not asking your ego to step down permanently, just to observe for a few moments. Listen to your soul. What is *it* seeking?

Write down the things in your life that you've worked the hardest for and honestly acknowledge if they feed your ego or your soul. Do this without blame. Just be honest and then ask yourself if you'd like to continue on that same path or if you are open to finding a new one. What would it look like to honor what your soul is seeking and to release a void that will never be filled?

CHAPTER FIVE

OWL

ONE MORNING, I FOUND AN owl feather in my backyard just lying in the grass. I tuned in and thanked the owl for the gift of their feather. I've lived in the same place since 1996 and have never found an owl feather, so this one is indeed a rare gift. It's not that an owl has never dropped one here, but I've never found one here before. To me, owls are amazing and somewhat mysterious with their silent flight, their amazing sight, their swiftness, and their ability to blend in with their surroundings and remain virtually unseen. The fact that they live on every continent except Antarctica means that nearly all humans know about owls and have them somewhere nearby. I believe this particular owl reached out to me in order to connect with us and remind us of another thing we humans have in common . . .

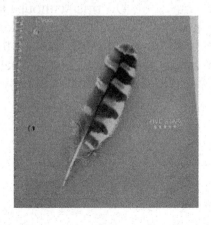

MESSAGE FROM OWL

There are so many clues that we leave for humans. [Things] to capture your imagination, [to] daydream [about], and [to help you] see the possibilities that are right there for you, just waiting to be taken. It's true that each species has certain qualities for you to connect with. We carry messages, signs, and connections to your heart that will assist you on your path. At our soul level, we want to help. We're all connected, right? In our physical manifestations, we know to be wary of you. Even those of you who love us could also be the ones that capture us and confine us. There are those of us that have offered our freedom to help teach you and open [your] hearts. Even though they knew what they were doing, it doesn't make it any easier. It also doesn't mean that they want it to continue. Yes, I gifted you a feather this morning and I could feel your excitement and gratitude! We're all connected, and I can also feel the longing, the desire for humans to have more of that connection, to learn and grow, to evolve into your higher [selves]. And yes, all that can be done without the death of your body.

All of us have the opportunity to have the intense, profound experience of expansion and connection to *all*. What would life look like if all of us were walking in both worlds? Totally connected to the here and now of everyday life—being able to work, pay the bills, travel, be with friends and family. But also being totally connected to the spirit self. That part of *all* of us that welcomes the unity, that embraces all that is, without judgment or wishing it were different. What if I told you that it's not only possible but it's the biggest part of making sense of why we're here?

We [nonhumans] see the sadness, the struggle, the addictions, the anger, the violence, the divisiveness, and *we* understand the purpose. We're viewing all that without emotion. Of course, we wish humanity didn't have to learn and heal and grow by being in pain or causing pain. That's where humans are at, though. And there are so many of you willing to take the leap and go beyond what has been for so, so long. Many of you are waking up and wanting more—not more stuff but more substance. More depth. More meaning. And we are here to assist in that evolution. We are here to honor our own [souls' paths], and yours, too. We [the animals] chose to come here [on Earth] with a deeper connection to the Source [of life and purpose], and humans chose to come here [in our human bodies] to find the path that leads you back to that Source. There's a part of every human that knows it's there, that draws you to it. Each of you, though, chooses a different way to find and walk that path.

[We pause for a bit.]

What do you see when you close your eyes? If you let your mind wander, where does it go? Where your mind goes is a clue as to where your soul is going. Those who believe that the mind is in charge and is seeking the highest good for the soul will continue to be happy with where it wanders. For those of you who believe the *heart* is more in tune with what you seek for your soul and its highest good, then you'll appreciate listening more to what it says and shows you. What do you see when you close your eyes and listen to your heart? I guarantee that when you see what your heart shows you, your wanderings will be far more satisfying to your soul and will help you navigate this existence.

Do you seek to be more connected, more in tune, more aware, more awake? Then close your eyes and let your heart speak to you. It is the conduit from your higher self, and it will be far more helpful to you than your mind could ever dream of being. Breathe into your heart, pull the knowledge from Source into your physical being, and find the path that has always been there but has been hidden by your mind. Your mind is not to blame; it's the arrangement that was made. There is no blame at all. It is exactly how it was intended to be in order for you to take the next steps on this journey.

You came in [to this world] knowing and remembering, and then [as you outgrew childhood] that knowing faded until you felt as if you knew nothing and were connected to nothing. Eventually, you want to remember, you want to re-establish the connection, and you listen to your heart. You hear, see, and feel the messages of love that are not your own; yet, somehow, they are. The connection is being strengthened and solidified, and you awaken what appears to be a "new you." That's when you realize it isn't new at all. It's the most real and authentic version of yourself, and it feeds you as you remember it's who you've always been. Shed the layers of the pretend you, and let your amazing true self be seen. Yes, let it be seen, and let it be your guide.

INSIGHTS

This message from Owl has so many different elements to explore. Evolving into our higher selves without the death of our body? What do we see when we close our eyes? Messages of love that are not our own, yet they are? Waking up and letting our souls guide us? I feel like we have been so limited in our experiences that we are somehow held back from finding our true selves or our true purpose for too long, but there always seems to be something that calls us to seek, to awaken. It seems strange that we come into this life remembering our connection and then forget it. I guess the good news is that we can remember and re-establish that connection! I love that Owl gives us a way to do that while also reinforcing why that longing to remember is so strong with some of us and why we keep seeking answers. It sounds like it's our soul guiding us to remember and awaken.

CONSIDERATIONS

What do you see when you close your eyes and let your mind wander? Just notice what you see or what you feel. Where is it leading your soul? Is that where you want to be heading?

Ask yourself how you feel about the idea of evolving into your higher self while still alive. Does it bring you joy, fear, wonder, disbelief, a mixture of emotions? Sit with that concept or journal your thoughts and feelings about it. Envision what your life would look like as an evolved being. How different is it from what your life looks like now?

What happens when you allow yourself to listen from your heart? Are you able to hear the messages that take you outside of your ego and your physical self? What is it that your higher self is saying to you? Breathe, relax and follow the knowledge and the messages that may feel new and yet are familiar.

CHAPTER SIX

CHEETAH

WHEN I WAS IN FOURTH grade I was tasked with doing a report on cheetahs. I'm not sure if I knew much about them before that, but I gained so much respect for them by the time I was done. In my young mind, it was fascinating how cheetahs ran so much faster than any other animal. Many years later, I learned how endangered they had become and how limited their gene pool was becoming, with only an average of 5 percent surviving in the wild. It made me sad to think that one day the only place they would be alive was in zoos, that those cheetahs would never have the opportunity to run and be free.

It's this kind of situation that makes me wish I could turn things around and make it better. I don't know if that's possible or not, but I do hope that there will always be cheetahs living and breeding in the wild. I'm not sure I want to live in a world without them running free.

MESSAGE FROM CHEETAH

People wonder if I'm more [catlike] or doglike. I don't fit into any category perfectly. What if we're not supposed to? Does everything need to be neat, tidy, packaged perfectly so everyone knows where everything belongs? I'm living proof that doesn't have to be. I don't fit in where I'm supposed to, and yet, here I am. Think about the humans who don't fit [into] someone else's category. Do they need to? Who wrote that rule? Why is that a thing? What if there were no labels at all? What if we just had a name but not a descriptor? Can you feel the judgment melting away? Can you feel the freedom coming in? Why did the separation begin at all?

The more labels we place on others, the more separation is created. Yes, there's a sense of belonging when a category of humans gather and find solace and strength, but in the end, aren't you all humans? Why do you not find solace and strength in that? Go even further! Aren't we all light and energy? What does that mean? If I'm light and energy and you're light and energy . . . are we all the same? At our soul levels, yes. In the physical forms we wear, we do look different, eat differently, live in a different environment, and so on. Does this mean, though, that one of us doesn't deserve to be here because of that different physical form? It feels to me [that] so many of you are desperately trying to make others more like yourselves in order to reclaim [a] connection. Do you see what I'm saying? You want the unity, you crave it, but [you] don't know or acknowledge it. You just don't know how to make that happen unless you all look and think similar.

What if the connection you seek could be found not by looking alike, praying alike, and so on but by accepting the unity in your humanness and also in your light and [energy]? That way, no one has to change, no one is wrong, no one is making bad choices, no one needs to be killed—including nonhumans—in order to fit everyone into a category. Think about it. Really think about it. What is it that scares or offends you when someone is different from you? Do you think they're wrong? Or do you begin to question yourself and wonder if you're wrong? It's so much easier to blame them for being wrong than to admit maybe you're more intolerant than you thought. But there's no blame in that! You recognized something in yourself that can now be healed.

Let me explain it another way. Many of you attempt to destroy or discredit those that are not like you. Is that an attempt to remove differences in order to be alike? If you're all alike, then there are no conflicts, correct? Maybe, maybe not. Think about it, though. Even when you're together with like-minded people who fit [into] the same category as you, are you really all the same? Aren't there still differences? Appearance, size, shape, food preferences, et cetera. So you're all in the same category, yet still different. But you wouldn't consider killing them or making them leave because of their differences, correct? Is it possible for you to expand your tolerance of differences, thereby allowing others to be in their own category and live their lives without judgment from another category?

Is this beginning to sound a bit ridiculous to some of you? I hope so, because it is. And yet, to some, it isn't ridiculous at all. This concept may be so offensive or frightening, it could feel like their world is shattering. Might that actually be okay? If your world is not big enough to include treating other categories with respect, tolerance, or compassion, maybe shattering those walls is a good thing. Maybe this is an opportunity to envision a world where all categories exist regardless of large or small differences. What if, just what if, that could be possible? All life-forms living [as] they are, without conflict, competition, or a need to change the others.

My physical form may not truly be canine or feline, and yet, here I am, existing with you and honoring my path. Just to be clear, too, I honor your path, and I am anxiously waiting for the day when humans begin to honor all paths, not just those that are similar to their own.

INSIGHTS

Did you even know that cheetahs are somewhat doglike? I didn't. I had to look it up. I remember from my elementary school report that they do not have retractable claws like other big cats, but I didn't know they are not able to roar. Thank you, Cheetah, for educating me.

I absolutely love this message about acceptance and tolerance. I'd never before even thought about anyone's intolerance being a way to create inclusion and safety. But now that Cheetah shared it, it makes sense. It also makes me wonder if that's something that can be unlearned. I'd like to think so. What if we only had names but no descriptors, like Cheetah said? How could that change the way we view things? To me, I can definitely see the freedom in that. I can also imagine for some, though, that it wouldn't feel like freedom at all. I know some humans who enjoy the safety of knowing what category they fit into and also—supposedly—knowing who else is in that category with them. The idea of tearing down those walls and removing the safe boundaries of categories may very well feel like chaos or torture. So do the categories get assigned by each of us, or do we just settle into one by default?

Maybe that's one reason I confuse or challenge some people: they can't figure out my category and see me almost as an alien that doesn't fit in anywhere. Without meaning to, I push their boundaries and possibly even question their own category. Cheetah's message is really making me think about the impact I might be having on others—and it might not be a pleasant one. How can I be me, being category-less, without causing too much disruption to others? Or am I supposed to be challenging others?

Envisioning a world where "all life-forms living [as] they are, without conflict, competition, or a need to change the others" makes my heart and soul happy. The idea of each one of us being able to be exactly who we are without fear of discrimination, abuse, ridicule, or death feels like the path to perfection.

CONSIDERATIONS

Where do you find solace? What makes you feel safe? What would you say your "category" is? Write your answers down and then look at what that list shows you—without judgment. At this point, you are who you are, and now you're just noticing it. Each one of us most likely has several boxes that we could label for ourselves. Look at each one and notice how you feel as you read it. Does it still serve you, or is it something that you can now let go of? Is it a label you've given yourself, or one that someone else gave you?

Write down situations, people, or places that make you feel uneasy, angry, or unsettled. Ask yourself why—again, without judgment. Just notice what could be causing these feelings. When you notice that you've put a label on someone else, ask yourself why. Does the label increase or decrease separation and understanding?

Make a list of ways in which you could be more accepting and tolerant. Where do you limit yourself from seeing another person's perspective? Does it seem too scary or too unnecessary to find value in a category different from your own? Look within to see if you're able and willing to take on just one "category" that you normally would avoid and see if you can be more tolerant and accepting.

CHAPTER SEVEN

HIPPOPOTAMUS

HIPPO WAS THE FIRST TO open the door to what I could be, something that has made me more connected to my higher self than I ever thought possible. After Dr. Jeri Ryan had helped me communicate with my dog Joey, I took her animal communication class and Hippo was the first one that I connected with telepathically. I can still vividly remember how I felt when I tuned in to Hippo. It felt completely different from speaking to a human or even daydreaming. I was connected to something outside myself that I didn't even know was there but that felt instantly familiar. It felt more real and genuine than most of the conversations I've had with humans. It felt clear, honest, kind, and deeper than what I was used to with most humans. And it happened in a matter of minutes, not months or years of building trust. While Joey was the catalyst to bring me to this moment, Hippo was the one who I *listened to* for the first time and who opened my heart to more awareness of this new path.

Years ago, I taught a class on animal communication and handed out pictures of some of the wolves from Wolf Haven International, where I volunteered for almost eight years. Each person then tuned in to a different wolf so they could communicate. When it was time for each person to share what they had experienced, one woman held back - she would start to speak up, then change her mind and be quiet; she would look at me expectantly and then look away. I could tell, though, that she wanted to share so I pushed her a little. She told me that I would think she was crazy, but I'm probably the last person who would think that of anyone! So she shared that she had heard flute music, and she was convinced it meant she had done something wrong. I asked her which wolf she had, and she told us that she was talking with Solo, a female who was kept to the back of the sanctuary.

I smiled and said to her, "You're not crazy at all. My sister gave me a flute for Christmas, and I was too shy to play it anywhere a human could hear me so I took it out to the sanctuary and stood outside Solo's enclosure to play."

The woman had tears streaming down her face and kept repeating, "I talked to a wolf, I talked to a wolf!" I remember having that exact feeling when I first talked with Hippo, and I was so thrilled to see it happen again.

MESSAGE FROM HIPPO

Greetings, Soul Mates and Earth Travelers. It's amazing, isn't it, how different we all are? Think of all the [shapes and sizes we come in] and roles we each fill. It's almost too much to fathom, and yet, it all works. We are all here to assist another in some way. We are all balance keepers for ourselves and for others, regardless of species. The circle of life image that many cultures embrace is true. There is no beginning, no ending, just the continuity of one being there for another. That may be difficult for some to take in. There are those who think only nonhumans are part of that circle, that humans are separate or more than nonhumans. Then there are those who think humans are interfering with the flow of this circle, that they're weighing it down and causing it to cease [moving]. Neither is accurate. It's a circle of life for *all* life, and one does not have the power to stop its movement. The circle continues its progression no matter what. Are there any easier or smoother progressions of the circle? Absolutely. But that doesn't mean it isn't moving. It isn't up to us to judge the movement.

We can, though, observe the movement and notice what it looks like. We can also make a choice to help it move more smoothly and easily. We can choose to travel a bumpy, uneven, dirty, difficult path, or we can choose to travel a smooth, even, clean, gorgeous path. It all comes down to observation. Once you observe—without judgment—the path you're on, you can then choose to continue [on] the same [path] or create a map to move from one path to another. Yes, observing where you are means looking at your life with honesty. Not to shame yourself for being where you are, just to acknowledge your location and choose if you like it or not. It's up to you to decide.

My hope is that you will only observe your path and not another's path. Also, [I hope] that you will not pass the responsibility of where you are on to another. You're being asked to dive deep, examine where you are with honesty and compassion, and then make a choice. Do you want to continue this path or look for another? The amazing part is it can be altered easily and with kindness. Changing paths does not have to be scary, unkind, or traumatic unless you choose it to be [so]. Yes, the responsibility is yours. Yes, your choices will most definitely impact others. With conscious observation and clear decision-making, it can be a smooth transition, one filled with happy excitement for a new beginning. Or you can wait or decide to stay where you are. You get to choose. The point is making your choice based on your honest observation and assessment.

Do you need some support? Call on one of us! We would love to offer support and encouragement. We're all connected at a soul level, and our souls want us to be happy, balanced, and on a loving path.

INSIGHTS

One thing Hippo is asking is for us to distinguish between judging and observing. This distinction gets more profound the more I consider it. I can totally see where I've been judging and then taking action on that judgment. How much more helpful and kind would it be for me to just observe? Sit with that for a moment—really feel the difference between judging and observing. Where do you feel it in your body? I can feel it in my heart. Judgment feels hard; there's a tightness and constricting feeling to it. Observing feels much softer; it feels more relaxed, and I can breathe more easily. I also notice that with observing, I don't really feel the need to do anything. I'm merely noticing what is. But with judgment, there's a sense of needing to fix or change it.

Conscious observation and clear decision-making . . .
Wow, that's another good lesson for me.

CONSIDERATIONS

Judge something and then observe the same thing. Notice how it makes you feel and what you think about. What kind of words do you use for judging versus observing? How do those words make you feel?

Now that you know what each one feels like, what have you judged that could be better served by observing? Think of family, coworkers, people who vote differently than you do, et cetera. How have you been judged in the past, and would you have felt more trust for the person if they had made an observation about you instead?

Do you see the circle of life as balanced and holding space for *all* life-forms? If not, who is excluded and why? Can you put your powers of observation to use and see if those life-forms can be included in the circle of life? Are you feeling resistance to including *all* life-forms? Ask yourself why that is, go deeper for the answer.

CHAPTER EIGHT

BAT

I HAVE ALWAYS LOVED BATS FOR some reason, even before I knew how beneficial they are to our ecosystem. It's amazing how they fly and navigate, and just the idea of a flying mammal is fascinating to me. A bat got trapped in my home years ago. I knew there was no way I could catch it, so I put my dogs in another room and then stood there watching the bat to see where it was trying to go. It was flying so close to me that I could feel my hair move as it flew around my head. There was no fear, though; I knew it wasn't trying to harm me. I ended up turning off all the lights and opening my door. The bat flew around my head a few more times and then went straight out the door to freedom.

When I was about eight or nine years old, my family took a trip to the Carlsbad Caverns in New Mexico. Part of the tour was to sit outside the opening to the cavern at dusk and watch as thousands and thousands of bats flew out and started to take care of the bug population. The sky was almost blocked out by the large number of bats. It was unlike anything I'd ever seen. It was then that I also learned about the balance of predators and prey. As the bats were beginning to go to work on keeping the bug numbers in check, so were the owls. They, too, were waiting for the bats, but not to be amazed as we humans were. They were waiting for their dinner. Yes, I'm one of "those people" who doesn't like to watch the reality of an animal being killed, even when it enables another one to live. What does it say about me that I'm okay watching bats eat bugs but not so much watching owls eat bats? Does that make me a speciesist? I guess so.

MESSAGE FROM BAT

It's obvious, isn't it? We're all learning from one another. All of us. Everyone is teacher and student. Everyone.

I use my heightened senses to make my way through the world. I don't have to think about it. Your scientists are finally discovering that your heart, not your brain, is your information center. Yet, still so many depend on thought processes to make their way through the world. Yes, we all need our brains, of course. Many of you are being called to find your way by listening to your heart. Your heart doesn't lie. It can't. Your brain, though, can and does.

Each one can choose what they teach and learn. Are you teaching love, tolerance, kindness, graciousness, gratitude, compassion? Or are you teaching hate, blame, shame, intolerance, greed? Ask yourself how you navigate your own life. Be honest with yourself about what you're teaching and what you're learning. Then see if that makes your heart happy or not. If not, then what are you able to shift to make your heart happy?

Oh, dear humans . . . You have tried for so long and so hard to make the paths you've chosen the *right* paths. Your head just won't consider that maybe it's time to try something else. How many have been killed to prove this? How many more need to be killed before you will listen to your heart centers and find a new path? One that might not require wars, hate, killing, and so much judgment. There are those of you who have attempted to alter or change the path of humanity— so far unsuccessfully. We have not given up on any of you! Nor will we. We will continue to honor our paths, all while sending you messages in the hopes that these messages will be heard by those of you who are able to create change. As you just read those words, what image came to mind? A politician? A famous person? A very wealthy person? Those are not [the people whom] I'm referring to. I am referring to each individual. Yes, each one of you has the power to effect change. It may not be a global impact immediately, but it could be after a bit of time passes. You have the power and the ability to create shifts and movement for humanity to be far more connected to *all* that is. You do! I want you to trust me, and I also want you to trust what your heart is telling you as you read these words.

We're not expecting any of you to make drastic changes. That isn't necessary and may not even be helpful. You can, though, make numerous, small adjustments to how you think, how you react, how you help or don't help, how you choose to be more aware, how you choose to be kind and tolerant. Do you see how easy it is? It won't cost you anything, except listening to your heart. It doesn't matter what anyone else does. You, though, can be aware and use [the] heightened senses that you may not know you have. You've always had them and had access to them. Tap into them now if you choose to, and feel the connection. Feel me sending you love and encouragement.

INSIGHTS

Does the concept of each of us being both teacher and student shift anything for you? Does it bring you a sense of freedom knowing you're not expected to figure things out all on your own? Or does it bring about a sense of unease thinking that you will need to place your trust in someone besides yourself? For me, it brings a sense of balance and it helps me see my path with more compassion and understanding. When I think back to the times when I felt I wasn't doing enough or having enough of an impact, I can now see that those were times when I was in the "student mode" and strengthening my skills and my resilience. Even while writing this book, I shamed myself for taking more than fifteen years after the concept came to me to get it down. It's easier to see how certain things needed to happen to prepare myself for this book, and also for a time when more people would be open to the concept.

The message from Bat about trying so hard to make our path the right path resonates with me, as well. I look back at the history of humans, and I have often struggled with the fact that while our technology has improved greatly, humans really haven't. We're still fighting wars over the same things. We still don't seem to be any more forgiving or tolerant than our ancestors were. How many people need to be killed before we finally accept that what we've been doing for thousands of years—maybe more—is not solving anything? Do you think it's possible that we can help create a shift? I bet we could!

CONSIDERATIONS

Make a list of the times in your life when you have been the teacher and the times when you have been the student. Keep in mind that this is probably not going to be obvious classroom settings. One of my biggest lessons involved rescuing Joey and learning not only something that I hadn't known existed but something that completely altered my path and opened up opportunities to continue learning and teaching.

Are you able to identify any areas in your life where you've shamed yourself? For not knowing enough, not doing enough, not being enough? Is Bat's message able to help you let go of that shame and see that you could have been in a student phase and didn't yet have the skills needed to teach?

You have the power and the ability to create shifts and movement for humanity to be far more connected to all that is. Does this statement from Bat ring true for you? If so, why? What actions could you take—or are you already taking—that will create shifts in our world? If not, why not? What about this statement makes you think or feel that it isn't possible? What limitations do you perceive that are preventing you from creating shifts?

CHAPTER NINE

NORMAN THE DOG

NORMAN IS THE DOG WHO currently shares my life with me, and as you can see, he is adorable! In 2013, an EF5 tornado hit the vicinity of Moore, Oklahoma, causing two billion dollars of damage, including the major destruction of two schools and more than three hundred homes. It also killed twenty-four people. After the disaster, I volunteered with American Humane to help care for the animal survivors in an emergency shelter. I flew out there and was working with the feral cats and cats with feline immunodeficiency virus (FIV). A few days after I had arrived, they brought in the last of the "tornado dogs" from the Moore Animal Shelter and put them in a quarantine area. The other volunteers working with the dogs spent all day cleaning crates and walking the dogs. Since I certainly wasn't taking the cats for walks and feral cats wanted nothing to do with any of us, I had extra time, so I offered to help care for these quarantined dogs.

As soon as I saw Norman, I was immediately drawn to him. He was so amazing and unique, he was just irresistible to me. He had some Shar-Pei features like a large muzzle and a wrinkled head, but he also had this gorgeous long reddish coat that looked nothing like a Shar-Pei. I'd never seen another dog like him at all. He was very interested in everything going on around him, but he was also extremely scared of humans when he was outside his crate. Each day I would do my chores, walk all the other quarantine dogs, and then spend a few extra minutes with Norman. I'd sit on the grass, and he would move as far away as he could while on his leash, not wanting me to pet him. I'd hold out my hand and talk to him, telling him that he was safe. Eventually, he started to let me barely touch him under his chin, and then after a bit, when I'd pull my hand back just a little, he'd take a half step toward me for a little more. I was thrilled! He was so brave, and I was so proud of him. I was in love with this dog!

I also knew that he could have a family out there looking for him. He didn't have any tags on his collar and didn't have a microchip, but that didn't mean he didn't have a family. I made the decision that if no one claimed him, I would adopt him and bring him home to Washington state, where I currently live. But my volunteer time had ended, which meant that I had to fly home and leave him there. Oh the guilt! I told him that he would either find his family or he and I would see each other again. Either way, it would be a happy ending for him. I was crying and so sad to leave him, not knowing if I'd ever see him again. Thankfully for me, after the shelter went through all the processes to reunite humans with their animals, no one claimed him, and I was able to bring him home! To me, the emergency shelter, which was set up in the town of Norman, Oklahoma, represented new beginnings and healing for the animals and the community that had lost so much. And that is why my sweet angel is named Norman.

MESSAGE FROM NORMAN

Try to imagine what life would be like without animal companions. For a lot of you, that feels sad, lonely, incomprehensible even. We have chosen to be of service and to come into your lives to help you remember how worthy of love you are. Were you expecting something else? [He smiles.] Whether you believe it or not, this is one of our main purposes. One of the many gifts we give is to help humans remember how worthy of love they are and how capable they are of passing that on to another. We help show you how to *be* in every moment, how to embody unconditional love. We do this for you, and we do it so that once you truly believe it, you'll do it for another. We are here to help you feel.

Whether we are domestic or wild, captive or free, anyone who sees us has the opportunity to choose how we make [them] feel. I feel your hesitation. Trust me and come with me. You get to choose how you feel when you see any animal. What do you feel, and why? Ask yourself, "Why am I feeling this way?" Not just happy animals but wounded, lonely, scared, tortured animals, too. Does it make you feel sad, angry, hopeless, lost, helpless? Good! Feel that, and then ask why. Why do you feel this way? What is it about you that feels what you feel? What is it about you that maybe doesn't allow yourself to feel anything? That's an even deeper question. How many [people] turn away at the sight of something unpleasant? What if you could look with your heart and reach out to *their* hearts? What if, by connecting to [an] animal and not turning away, you give it hope? Could you send a message to that animal that humans are able to go to the dark places in order to help another? What if you could actually stop the abuse and suffering by seeing it, not avoiding it?

Do you see where I'm going? Can you imagine what it would be like for thousands and thousands of you to send love and gratitude to wounded, suffering animals? Do you feel the shift? Do you see how [by] standing firm in your commitment to help another, you actually do?

Let me explain it another way. Let's say you see an animal not being treated well by its person. Let's say it's a farm animal that is being forced to work too hard and is clearly struggling. You see the human shouting at it to do more, go faster. What do you feel? Rage toward the human? Sadness for the animal? How have you helped that animal? What if you could send love and gratitude to that animal instead? Would that help the animal? Would that help the animal be able to see that not all humans are scary or mean? Could you also be helping the human? Where does their anger come from? Why are they mistreating their animal to begin with? Could you make a choice to add love or compassion to the situation? Is that a possibility? I think we can all agree that there's already enough anger and sadness going on—no need to add more to it. I'm not at all condoning violence or causing suffering. I'm also not saying that you should be happy about witnessing suffering. But if you're not in a position to remove that animal from the situation, how can you help? Do you turn your back on them in order not to feel? Or do you look at them and fill them with love? Your love may be the only good thing that happens to them. Do you see how [that] could shift everything? Can you give that animal and that human gratitude for helping you find more compassion than you thought you were capable of? I realize that this may be a stretch. Start slowly, then. Love the animals that make you sad or hopeless. Help them see what a *good* human looks like and feels like. You can still feel sorrow that they're where they are, but haven't you also brought balance to their lives by loving them and being grateful to them?

INSIGHTS

Oh, Norman . . . This really makes me ponder. I admit I'm one of those people who can't change the channel on the TV quickly enough when I see commercials about abused and neglected animals. But even though all those animals in the ads have long since been rescued and cared for—and since we're all connected—couldn't it still be helpful to send them love and gratitude? I think it could. What about the livestock you see on the freeways being shipped in trucks and crates? Honestly, it makes me so sad. But like Norman said, how am I helping those animals by looking away and being sad?

Is it possible for me to send them love and gratitude and at least feel like I've done something helpful? I will still be sad, but it would be balanced with the knowledge that I did something.

For me, the sadness comes from a sense of helplessness when I see these sorts of things. But if I believe what all the animals are telling us, that we're all connected, then I'm not really helpless at all, am I? I have the ability to reach out to them on a different level and give them hope, let them see another side of humans. It's not within my ability to rescue them and let them all run free on some amazing farm, but I can do *something* to help. And from now on, I will.

Since this conversation with Norman, I have actually been making myself watch the sad advertisements. At first, it was very difficult, but I've realized that I do feel differently when I honor them. I take a breath, send them love, and envision them happy, healthy, and loved. I haven't changed the past at all, but I have done something. And that "something" is sending them the message that not all humans are scary or will cause them harm.

CONSIDERATIONS

Do you see yourself as worthy of love? If you have a pet, do you believe that they are correct and you are as amazing as they think you are? What would it take for you to believe them and bring into your being the truth that you are, indeed, worthy?

What animal-related situations create feelings of rage, anger, sadness, hopelessness, or helplessness for you? In any of these situations, do you have the ability to rescue them or remove them from the situations they're in?

How can you move beyond the feelings listed previously and send love, hope, and gratitude to these animals? What about test animals in research facilities?

You might not be able to rescue them, but could you begin to buy a product from a company that does not test on animals? Could you also send a message to the company itself to tell them why they are no longer getting your money? What about the destruction caused to orangutan habitats in the processing of palm oil? Is it an option for you to only give your money to the companies that sustainably source their palm oil?

CHAPTER TEN

PRINCESS ANGELINE THE ORCA

PRINCESS ANGELINE (J17) WAS A member of the resident J Pod of orcas in the Pacific Northwest. She died at the age of thirty-nine and was a mother of four and a grandmother of three. You may have heard of her daughter Tahlequah (J35). Tahlequah was the mother orca, who in 2018, swam more than a thousand miles in seventeen days while carrying her dead calf on her nose, mourning the loss of her offspring. It's a sad and fascinating story, and while this garnered worldwide attention, there remains much to do in order to help the struggling orcas survive and be healthy. The amazing news though, is that in September of 2020, Tahlequah gave birth to a healthy orca calf!

I came to "know" Princess Angeline while working with my "We Are the Walrus" Power of Eight group. We came together while taking a one-year class with Lynne McTaggart, an American alternative-medicine activist, lecturer, journalist, author, and publisher. Every week our group gets together online and follows Lynne's Power of Eight program to bring about healing and balance. It was during one of our intentions that Princess Angeline showed up for me. We were sending an intention to bring love, hope and healing to the orcas, and I remember her presence, her grace, her intelligence, and her incredible power. I was in awe. I hadn't known her name or what pod she belonged to at that time, but I vowed to find out. I needed to know more about her.

Since then, Princess Angeline shows up every so often to add her wisdom, her grace, and her inspiration to our group. She has become especially connected with one of my friends in the group, Nancy. The two of them have had an amazing journey together, one I believe will continue for many more years.

MESSAGE FROM PRINCESS ANGELINE

Dear ones, I must begin by telling you that as you read my words, I am with you, and I'm overjoyed to be connecting with you. As an orca, I was able to make an impression on humans, on the water and all that is in the water.

Slow down for just a bit here . . .

Feel your heartbeat . . .

Feel your breath. Feel the rise and fall of each breath . . .

Feel the connection to our Mother we call Earth . . .

Feel me with you and feel you with me. It goes both ways, and each one feels different, doesn't it?

See if you can feel the blackness of the world just outside of the one you're in. You will not get lost, I promise it.

Feel me as I close the gap. Did you just realize that there is no gap? [She smiles.] Does it make you wonder how it's possible? Does it make you wonder how you haven't noticed it before? Does it make you wonder what else there is? Good, dear ones, good. Keep wondering, keep wandering, keep seeking, keep trusting those feelings you have that tell you there is so much more than our conscious brains know. Those feelings are your soul remembering where we came from, why we're here, and what the next steps could be. Even though there is no gap—we're all connected—we each have different paths, different experiences, and different promises to keep. Yet, even though they're different for each of us, they will bring us all closer and closer to each other and to a path that not only remembers but rejoices in the way we have traveled to get there. You are beautiful, you are amazing, and you are here for a very specific and valuable reason. As am I and all the others.

Oh, dear ones, I'm excited for you as you take these next steps, and I am so grateful to be connected to you again. I say "again" because you're on your way to remembering that there never was any separation at all. Your path is perfect, your path is necessary, your path matters tremendously, and your path is why you're here. Are you wishing your path has been different? Please do not. You wouldn't be right here, right now, if it had been different. You are needed, your soul is needed, and you know that. When you slow down and feel your heartbeat, when you connect with the gap that does not exist, you know this to be true. Knowing this truth feeds you and brings you closer and closer to remembering more and more and more in order to share with others. I have never left, none of us has. Shape-shift with me and the others, and feel the connection, the unity, and the pure love that we all are.

INSIGHTS

Princess Angeline's graciousness and her calm, accepting nature comes through so well in her message, and I very much hope you can feel it as you read her words. Part of me thinks she needed a whale body in order to hold her enormously kind and loving soul. The other part, though, knows it would be just as strong and amazing if she had been in the body of a mouse. I find myself becoming calmer and calmer when I read her message, and also when I just think of her. I love that she has given us a step-by-step way to connect with her, close "the gap that isn't there," and then knowingly reconnect.

I took Princess Angeline up on her offer to step into the blackness and reconnect with her, and it was amazing. I felt my soul and hers together in a way that was strong and real in both worlds. It felt as if my physical hearing became stronger, and I was hyperaware of every sound around me—every bird chirping, every dog barking, every child laughing, and even the different sounds of the wind as it gently rippled through each tree around me. I could also feel us both in the blackness that was most certainly not a void; it was full of energy and life. I will most definitely be joining up with her there again!

CONSIDERATIONS

If you are interested, follow her guidance and step outside of yourself and connect with her. Just feel what it feels like and notice how your body and soul react to being in her presence.

Do you wish your path had been different somewhere along the way? See if you can give yourself permission just to be grateful for being exactly who you are right now.

Continue to work with Princess Angeline in connecting

and strengthening the connection to *all*. Journal about your experiences with her and also changes you notice, such as when you are calmer, more accepting, kinder to yourself and others, more grateful, et cetera.

CHAPTER ELEVEN

COUGAR

A S I WROTE THIS BOOK, I just knew that one of the animals would discuss the idea of intolerance among humans. I didn't know which animal it would be, but it turned out to be the cougar. Here in North America, cougars are the most efficient hunters. They can take down their prey in as little as fifty yards. They're very fast for short bursts, but they don't have the endurance to run for miles and miles, unlike wolves who can run after their prey for several miles, even hours. They've got a pack, though, and work in collaboration to bring down large prey. The cougar hunts alone and does it very well. The cougar is also an important part of keeping our ecosystem balanced and certainly has a valuable place in this world.

This conversation with Cougar was one I did not expect and am still pondering the full implications of. It's not that I really knew what any of the animals would share, but this one with Cougar goes beyond what I thought could be shared.

MESSAGE FROM COUGAR

Let's talk about intolerance and judgment, shall we? My kind has been judged for being who we are—predators. I realize that logic tells us we need both predator and prey to keep the balance, but people seem to be intolerant of us predators. Is it because you fear us? Do we challenge your ego in some way? We all know that hardly any human could overcome one of my kind without some sort of weapon. Is that why we are killed and not tolerated or allowed to be who we are?

You need us to help keep the balance, and yet you want to eliminate us and other predators. Is it really an ego that can't handle being challenged, that makes some of you want to kill so much? We see your bloodlust, we see how you manipulate things to make it easier and easier to kill, we see that the appetite for killing—even to the point of extinction—is never satisfied. Yet, you keep doing it. We know that you kill prey, too, not just predators. We realize that there are many humans who wonder what all the killing is about, too. It used to make sense. It was survival. Now it appears to be sport or fun or a way to prove your dominance. But wouldn't it run its course at some point? How many humans need to prove that by killing an animal they are somehow dominant? At what point will humans leave the old—and unnecessary—ways behind? Very few of you actually need to hunt to survive.

So is it really sport, or is there something else going on? Do those of you who kill for fun wish you could kill humans, too? Would you kill a human if there were no punishment? How far removed do you think today's humans are from your ancestors thousands of years ago? Were they more evolved since they hunted to survive? Or are you more evolved since you've created weapons that make killing easier and you hunt for fun?

Before you go getting defensive, stay with me. This ties in directly with how you treat each other. There are some of you who have no desire to kill and also no desire to judge another because they don't look like you. There are so many, though, that still do judge and treat those who are different [badly]. Why do you think that is? You've named it *racism*. Go deeper, though. Why? Why do so many fear others who are different? Why do so many others not fear those same humans?

Please know that the message I'm about to give is for those [who feel] the need to cause harm to another, including murder. This is a different distinction from those who are intolerant, uneducated, unaware, or [treat] others [the way] they [were taught] to. Could there be something left over from your ancient ancestors? Could this be a trigger that says your life is in danger of anything that looks different? Could this be a defense mechanism? If that's true, then how does that mechanism get turned off or evolve not to see other humans as a threat or dangerous to you? Is it only with future generations [that can change]? I doubt that, but it's possible. Perhaps humans could learn to alter that defense mechanism themselves. What if you didn't have to wait for many more generations until that now-defective gene no longer exists? What if you could turn it off today? You can.

[I see a DNA strand with an anomaly in it. That is the part to be removed.]

What if your scientists and healers could locate [it] and remove it? Can you see now why all the logic and conversation and facts are irrelevant? One side cannot understand the deep hatred, and the other side cannot understand why there is no fear or hatred. It's simple biology. You are what you are. Just as I am. The difference is, though, that I don't judge others as being worthy or not worthy of living. I kill to survive and to protect my territory. And since my evolution is essentially functioning well for me, I don't need to alter my DNA to protect others.

Humans, you are evolving into your higher selves. Not all, though, are with you on this path. Use your science and technology to improve your functioning rather than building bigger, smarter weapons. There will never be a weapon large enough to satisfy an unbalanced ego or to appease outdated DNA. The struggle will just continue. Look for another path to address the cause, seek to find an answer that benefits all. Seek answers that help, not harm. Your aggression, anger, and violence have served you for quite some time now. You are shifting, though, and now is the time to find new ways to serve your journey.

For those humans who are not willing to kill another for their differences but do still judge them or treat them poorly, [you] can be healed, as well. It's so easy to just keep doing what you learned to do as you grew up or [to do] what others around you are doing. You can, though, choose to take another path that lets go of the judgment and the harm. Most of us have heard about the mirror effect: what bothers you in another is actually something that bothers you about yourself. If you are wanting to, you can ask yourself what it is about another that you are so intolerant of. Are you afraid that their differences will expose the fact that you're not being true to yourself? Do you think that if you are like all the others around you, you won't hear that quiet voice deep in your soul that is asking you to step out from behind the mask you've been wearing? Why do you believe there is only one way to be, to look, to love, to pray, to live? What part of you do you wish could be free of those constraints? [If] you looked within, what would you see? Do you see a beautiful soul worthy of love, acceptance, and compassion? If not, why not? Maybe you aren't able to give love, acceptance, and compassion to another since you don't give it to yourself.

I realize that to some, this sounds so simplistic. If you go deep enough and dig far enough for the answers, there's nothing simple about it all. It means stripping away every label you've ever given yourself and seeing the true you. The you that maybe has been hidden your entire life. The you that maybe is ready to step forward and see yourself and everyone else as worthy of honoring [. . .] no matter how different and as worthy of existing without apology or justification. Just . . . [be] . . . you.

INSIGHTS

I think it's important to ask ourselves why there are still so many intolerant people living in our world right now. But it's also important to consider why there are also so many people who are *not* intolerant in our world right now. If this is about evolution of the human species, wouldn't we all be intolerant in our own way? But we're not. So does that lend itself to the theory that we are evolving? And if we all have a right to be here and we all serve a purpose, does that also include those who are racist, homophobic, misogynistic, and completely intolerant?

As much as I hate to admit it, the answer is yes. But let's go even further and ask ourselves if we need to have those kinds of people around. I believe the answer is no. I believe they are here to teach us a lesson. I believe that we, as humans, are evolving into our higher selves. And I believe that we still have the people around that are intolerant, that are still violent, that are still causing harm because they are here teaching us a powerful lesson, one I hope that we truly learn very soon.

It may seem easy to judge another who we think deserves to be judged—those who cause harm to another, those who are racist, those who judge others unfairly. The bottom line, though, is that we're still judging them. And if the goal is to not judge, then does that mean we shouldn't be judging them, either? Even if we think we are justified in judging them? How do we shift from assigning blame and judging another to understanding why the situation is happening at all? Can we, as humans, look at another situation, another person, and instead of judging them, look at them openly and honestly and see what the lesson is? Or at least send them love and compassion, like Norman suggested? If we could let go of the judgment and the blame and shame, wouldn't we then allow space for ourselves not to need to be taught those lessons? Is that even possible?

It really does feel to me that humans are evolving and taking another step beyond where we were. Perhaps that is why we're seeing so many people digging their heels in and fighting to stay where they are. Even if they can't consciously acknowledge what's going on or articulate their feelings, do they still feel the shift? Are they still frightened by it? Can those of us who *are* looking forward to this shift, this openness, this tolerance, can we have compassion for those who are fighting against it? I realize that the word *fighting* probably isn't the right word, but that's what it feels like right now. There are scientists who believe that forty to fifty millions of years ago there was a species of the genus Miacis that eventually branched off, and one branch became feline while the other branch became canine. Eventually, that original species ceased to exist, leaving just canine and feline. Could that be happening with humans? What if humans today are facing a similar evolution? What if we are branching away from violence and hatred and intolerance and murder to actually becoming more compassionate, gentle, loving, aware humans?

It could explain why facts seem to be irrelevant to some people. I'm a mix of passion and pragmatism, and I will stand firm in my beliefs and fight for it unless I am presented with facts that lead me to a different conclusion. My logical brain does kick in and say, "Oh there's something I didn't know, but now that I know it, I will form a new opinion based on those facts." But it's always been frustrating to me to see that some people still refuse to see the truth, even when presented with facts and data. They refuse to budge from their positions, their opinions, and they will strongly defend those opinions, regardless of the proven facts right in front of them. Could it be that I was judging them as being unwilling to see the facts or unwilling to look at things without emotion? Could it be that they were unable to process a change of heart, or accept a new truth? What if humans truly are evolving into our higher selves and those of us who are welcoming were to have more compassion for those who fear it?

When Cougar talked about there somehow being an anomaly in our genetic structure, part of me was afraid to actually put that in this book. But I vowed to honor what the animals told me, so I kept it in. And I'm glad I did, because what if Cougar is right? What if we could see that anomaly and help those who are willing to change? And if that's not an option, could those of us who don't have that anomaly, have compassion for those who do? The part of me that is kind and tolerant understands that concept, and I believe I could have compassion for them—except for those who are causing harm. I still struggle with that part of it, that the injustice, intolerance, suffering, and violence needs to continue until we all learn. My pragmatic side understands why people, animals, and the environment are still being harmed. My passionate side, though, can barely stand the thought of it continuing. It hurts my soul to even think about.

Cougar clearly brings up some very difficult topics for discussion. But I'm hopeful that we can learn how to have these discussions with respect, listen to each other, and maybe even be open to hearing another person's point of view without trying to change their minds.

CONSIDERATIONS

Are there any animals that you think *deserve* to be killed? Are there any animals that you don't mind being killed (e.g. cows, pigs, chickens, et cetera)? Are there animals that you think humans should not be allowed to hunt (e.g. cats, dogs, endangered species, animals in confined spaces, et cetera)? Why or why not? Be honest. No one will know your answers. Why do we, as a society, place value on some animals but not others?

When you look at yourself, do you see a beautiful soul worthy of love, acceptance, and compassion? If so, has it always been that way, or was it something you've learned (or remembered)? If not, why do you think that is? What is stopping you from seeing yourself as worthy of love, acceptance, and compassion?

When it comes to humans who are different from you, regardless of the difference, what triggers you to judge them? For me, one of my triggers is when people don't protect the environment. When I hear someone support drilling in the Arctic or running an oil pipeline through Native lands, I am immediately triggered and judge them, assuming that they don't care about our water supply or what happens to people or animals. I admit that I assume they just don't care about future generations and what we'll be leaving them. Maybe I'm right, maybe I'm not, but is being triggered, assuming the worst, and judging them helping anything or anyone? Probably not.

CHAPTER TWELVE

RATTLESNAKE

PERSONALLY, I THINK RATTLESNAKES ARE beautiful. It doesn't mean I want to hold one or play with one, but I can definitely appreciate them and their role. Plus, they need to be out in the wild keeping things in balance. My father taught first aid and CPR while he was working for Escondido Fire Department, and he was the first certified CPR trainer/instructor in San Diego County. As a firefighter in Southern California, he saw plenty of rattlesnake-bite victims and did what he could to educate people about rattlesnakes and the best course of action if you are bitten.

I remember him teaching me and my sister that you could tell the age of a rattlesnake by the number of rattles on their tails. There are typically two or three rattles for every year of a rattlesnake's life (e.g. the one in the picture would be three to five years old), and most rattlesnakes live fifteen to twenty-five years. I also remember that an older rattlesnake can strike you and regulate how much venom they deliver, or choose not to inject any venom at all. Younger rattlesnakes, though, don't yet have that ability, and a strike from them usually delivers all the venom they have, potentially making them more deadly than an older snake.

The closest I've been to a wild rattlesnake was a little less than two feet. Luckily for me, though, it was very early in the morning and still quite cool out, so this particular rattlesnake was just waking up and moving more slowly than normal. But it was coiled up, and I wasn't able to see the tail. I just calmly backed away and gave it all the space it wanted. It was smelling the air with its tongue, which is the best way to describe how they use their tongues to collect chemicals in the air that evoke electrical signals in the brain. I still remember how gorgeous it was as it sat there and how amazed I was to be in its presence, even as I retreated from it.

MESSAGE FROM RATTLESNAKE

Hello, humans. My kind have been traveling this [Earth] for a very long time, and we have seen so many things change and so many things stay the same. Yes, it's true that all life-forms are connected. It's also true that some of us are a bit more removed, and for good reason. We came here as more solitary beings in order to observe, in addition to being on our own paths. We didn't come here to be food, clothing or companions to humans, and we are intentionally not safe to be around. There are some humans that would feed their ego by dominating or killing us, but this message is not for them. This discussion is for those of you that neither want to kill us nor want to share your lives with us— which ends up being most of you.

We live among you but go unnoticed for most of our lives. By doing so, one of the things we do is observe human evolution and pass that information on to our young. We can sense and feel those of you who are actively seeking to move beyond what humans have been for ages and ages. You are the ones who wish to be different from what most humans are. You are seeking to be more deeply connected to *all* and to find more meaning while you're here. We see those who are perfectly happy not digging too deep, and we do not judge or wish they were any other way. They are walking their paths just as they're meant to, and it brings them comfort. Then we see those of you who consider that path to be unbearable or unthinkable. And for you, it is. You're here to expand the boundaries and create new paths—for yourselves and for others.

Neither group is right nor wrong. There is no right or wrong. Can you imagine if every human were seeking to go more deeply and expand the boundaries? At first, it might seem like a good idea. But take another look at it and see how chaotic and troublesome it could be. It would be like every one of you driving your cars at the same time without any rules or road signs at all. Some would lead. Some would follow. Most, though, would just be all over the place causing others to either have an accident or divert them from their own path to get out of the way. There's a reason you're not all doing the same things and in the same ways. It's intended to be this way. So instead of seeing someone who is perfectly fine where they are and judging them or labeling them in a negative way, could you instead just accept that they are doing exactly what they came here to do? Even if you don't understand or agree with it. When you use your focus and energy judging another, you're learning a lesson, of course. You're also detracting from your own path, deviating, if you will, from where you intended to be. You're allowed to deviate all you want, of course. Is that in your highest interest, though? Might you be serving your higher self more by keeping your focus and your energy on the path you're on?

INSIGHTS

Okay, this is a completely new concept for me—that we're not all here to push ourselves, to go deeper, to grow and evolve. I need to sit with this for a bit and contemplate it because it seems contrary to everything I thought I knew. I appreciate the distinction between those humans who want to kill and those that don't. In the group that doesn't want to kill are those who are striving to be different from humans of the past and also those who are here happy where they are. I have often wondered how some people seem to lead "charmed" lives when I seem to struggle so much more. Could it be that it's not about judging one path as charmed and another as a struggle but being open to accepting that they're just two different paths? When I look at it that way, it does really change my perspective—for them, and for me! It becomes less about "they're doing it right and I'm doing it wrong" to "they're honoring their path and I'm honoring mine."

Wow. Thank you, Rattlesnake!

The idea, too, that it may not be the best idea for us all to be evolving at the same time needed to be processed, as well. It seems like us all healing and evolving would be a good thing. The more I sit with it, though, the more I see Rattlesnake's logic. When I look at my own healing and evolution, it hasn't been pretty or easy or smooth. It has been rough, painful, and challenging, *and then* rewarding. I can see now how having us heal in stages actually brings more balance to us all.

CONSIDERATIONS

What if there are also humans who are here to be more solitary? Is that a possibility to consider and be open to?

If you could trade "skins" with Rattlesnake for just a few moments, what would you see when you looked at humans? What would you see when you looked at your own life? Can you see what you have accomplished just by honoring the path you came to honor, even if it's not like someone else's?

Is there someone in your life who you have judged unfairly? Are you holding them accountable for failing to walk a path that isn't theirs? Are you able to let go of giving them your focus and your energy and give it to yourself instead?

CHAPTER THIRTEEN

JOEY THE DOG

IT'S ONLY APPROPRIATE THAT OUR last conversation is with the dog that started all of this for me—Joey. As I mentioned in the beginning, I rescued Joey after his person had passed away and one of his neighbors asked me if I could take him. I didn't know that he had been abused; I just knew he needed a home and that he and I connected. He was so incredibly happy to be petted and to just play. He would chase the ball for as long as I would throw it. I've never known a dog to be so happy running and playing. And when I would tell him what a good boy he was and how much I loved him, he would lean his head back, close his eyes, and soak it all in, every bit of it.

Very quickly, though, I realized that Joey had some issues and some behavioral problems that could be frightening. There were times when Joey and I would be playing and then, in an instant, he would begin snarling and charge me in full attack mode. I was able to escape every time without being mauled, but it scared me deeply. The strange thing was that once he had released all that rage, he was totally fine and wanted to play again. It was as if the attack hadn't happened at all. I, however, was not able to get over those incidents so quickly.

At the time, my nephew—who visited almost daily— was very young, and there were also other young children who lived nearby. I had been working with Joey, doing the best I could, but his issues were far beyond my skills at that time. I had reached out to the person who brought him to me and asked for more detail about what had happened to Joey. They told me that they had known he'd been abused but hadn't told me about it because they were afraid I wouldn't take him. They had tried several times to take Joey away from his abusive owner and even called the authorities but without any luck.

I came home one day and both my father's arms were bandaged up. Joey had gone after my nephew, and my father had been attacked trying to protect his grandson. I could no longer ignore that Joey was dangerous. I called a friend who had been helping me with Joey, and she referred me to an animal communicator in California. I called and left a desperate voice mail begging for help. She called me back that evening and introduced me to what telepathic communication was and how it worked. It resonated deeply with me, and I *knew* it was real. She talked with Joey, and we discovered that his abuse was more severe than we knew.

She shared with me what message Joey had given her. "I love where I am now," he told her, "I know I'm safe and loved for the first time. But I also know that I can't control what I do, and I can't be trusted. I know I hurt others but don't want to. I wish I could stay here but know that it's my time to go. I will always love Shawndra and be grateful to know what love feels like."

I was devastated. None of this was his fault! He was a good dog, but a human had taken away his chance at living out his life. The communicator and I discussed all the options at length, and in the end, I knew in my heart there was only one solution—the one he had asked for. Being with him while he died was the hardest thing I'd ever had to do up to that point in my life. The guilt and pain I experienced were more than I thought I could handle. Even now, knowing what I know, I still wish I could have done something different, but that was not how we were meant to travel our paths. He needed to be released from the pain he was suffering, and I needed to be pushed to the brink in order to seek deeper answers.

I did eventually talk with Joey, but it took me more than four years before I was able to move past the pain and be able to connect with him. Even though I was so incredibly grateful to him for the doors he had opened for me, I still felt the guilt over him needing to suffer in order for me to learn. I just wish that another soul didn't have to be harmed in order for me to learn and grow—or anyone for that matter. Then again, would I have worked so hard to find answers if I wasn't feeling so much pain and guilt? Honestly, probably not.

Once I connected with him and began the conversation, he helped me realize that besides teaching me, he was also honoring his own path, learning his own lessons. Of course! Even though we're all connected, we each still have our own path to travel. He wasn't holding on to any anger, regret, or bad feelings. He fully understood how and why our paths had crossed. I, however, had been beating myself up for more than four years over it all.

Joey helped me release the guilt and torment that I'd been carrying. He helped me understand things that my broken heart couldn't, or wouldn't, see. Honestly, it's still difficult for me to accept that humans learn such powerful lessons by someone else's suffering. My brain can grasp the concepts of connection, growth, feeling, going deeper into our souls. My heart, though, still wishes for it to be less painful. I'm still learning, and he's still teaching . . .

MESSAGE FROM JOEY

So many talk about love—what it means, how it impacts our lives and our decisions. Love is why each of us is here. Not just here in these bodies but here reading my words and connecting. Each of us seeks some sort of connection to another, human or nonhuman. As we connect, we discover more and more about ourselves and what our purpose may be.

Part of my path while on Earth as Joey was to learn to love under abuse. I did it. I learned what I needed to and so did my person, so he left. That's when I found [Shawndra], which led me to everyone who is connecting with me right now. If you each choose to, you can accept the love I have to offer, knowing, though, it is the same as the love you have to offer. Each of us came here to feel, to know love, and to give love. I can feel you searching for more than what you perceive and what you do each day. All of this—*all* of it—is being created in order to show us how to expand beyond what we thought our boundaries were. Can you remember a time when you were so deeply connected to Source, to each other, that all of you communicated with just your hearts [telepathically]? Can you now begin to imagine why so many feel lost, feel alone, feel disconnected, and are attempting to fill those empty feelings with external distractions? Each one is seeking the same thing for the most part, and each one is looking for the path that leads you back to the knowing and the connection. And since there isn't any sort of map, each one is finding [their] own way the best [they] can.

Do you think there are some who have found their way back? Yes, there are. Do you wonder why they don't come back and show others the way? Because they realize that no one can lead you back; it is a path that only you can travel. They can give clues, though—this book is one. The great hearts of healers that help you see beyond your limited vision are also giving you clues. Do you ever wonder if all this matters? Yes, it does. It matters to all every time anyone adds to your vibrational frequency or road map. Once you know certain things, you can't unknow them. They become part of you and help guide you.

INSIGHTS

The images Joey has shown me and the feelings he has shared with me all add to the depth of his words, and I realize that I'm not able to fully convey his message just by sharing the words. I wish I could share with you the enormity of his visions and the soul message he's sharing. He's suggesting we look at him and focus on the word *love*. Just breathe in and breathe out slowly and let the feeling of his love connect with you. Please do this before you continue reading.

A SECOND MESSAGE FROM JOEY

I'm sharing with each one of you how intense your love is, how connected you are, how aware you are, and how powerful the focus of love is. Take this focus of love, and let it heal all that you are ready to heal. Notice, though, that there may not be nearly as much to heal as you thought. When you are focused on love, does it change your perspective? Look at beings that are not being nourished with enough love or even food to sustain their bodies. Are you able to send them love? Can you step outside your perception of [lacking] and give them your love? Yes, you can all still strive for the vision of every human being safe, being fed, and having their needs met.

You can also amplify those effects by adding more and more love into all that you're doing. What about a loved one who is fighting a disease? What if you send them love, but they don't overcome that disease? Did it fail? Most certainly not. Maybe their path was not to overcome it, or maybe there was too much fear or doubt mixed in with your love and conflicting messages were sent?

The goal is to get to a place where you are able to fully and completely focus on love without a trace of fear, doubt, guilt, shame, anger, or desperation. Even if you only hold that focus for ten seconds, those ten focused seconds are far more powerful than twenty minutes of a partially focused mix of love and fear. Train yourself to know what it is you're feeling and also why. Be honest with what you feel and the names you give it. Be honest with your expectations of how quickly it will happen for you. This is not a competition; no one will know where you're at except you. If you find [you're] comparing [yourself] to another, that's just [an] awareness that you're not fully focused on love, and that's to be expected.

I was just one dog who loved the human who abused me and then loved the human who loved me. Keep pushing past the labels and the perceptions, and you'll find that they are both the same. Your ego wants to make one more admirable than the other, but it isn't. Look at the incredible love that came from both. Keep looking. You'll find it. I promise.

INSIGHTS

Oh my . . . I'm not even sure where to start. I had a feeling that his message would have a profound impact on me, I just didn't know how profound. Joey's message makes me think differently about all kinds of things. I could definitely feel myself shift as he was talking about being focused on love and then healing what is ready to be healed. I could feel some things that were ready to heal, but I was no longer consumed by them or caught up in the energy of them. I can understand why he would say that there may not be as much to heal as I thought, too. To me, it feels like there's still something there, but it's not as weighty as it was.

One thing that came up for me was how I had judged myself for not writing this book years ago. I realized that I had been shaming myself for not following through and not doing it as quickly as I thought I should have. But after hearing Joey's message, I can see how everything has happened exactly as it was meant to. I can really and truly let go of the shame, the guilt, the comparison—all of it—and realize that all along the way, I've been right where I needed to be, including right now.

I'm sure it's no surprise that Joey's message about remembering when we all used to communicate with our hearts, or telepathically, really resonates with me. I can't prove it, of course, but I do believe that humans used to be far more in touch with this type of communication, both with other humans and with nonhumans. As we separated ourselves from the nonhumans and from Mother Earth, I believe we began the process of forgetting how to connect at a heart level. We've made great strides in our technological advancements, but at what cost? It feels to me like some of us are serious about finding our way back to being more connected and more authentic.

I have to say, too, that I agree with him about how his abusive human and I both exemplify love. I haven't fully wrapped my head around it, but I'm close.

Joey's message gives me hope—hope for my path, your path, and Earth's path.

CONSIDERATIONS

Tune in and focus on *love*. Feel Joey sending you love, and just notice how it feels.

Get to a place where you are able to fully and completely focus on love without a trace of fear, doubt, guilt, shame, anger, or desperation, even if only for ten seconds. Train yourself to know what it is you're feeling and why.

Find a situation for yourself or someone else where you perceive the lack of something—money, food, health care, love, safety, et cetera. Intently focus on love, and become stronger and stronger at filling that situation with love.

CHAPTER FOURTEEN

CLOSING TIME

WHEN WE SHIFT OUR FOCUS, our awareness, to the love, the joy, the hope, the innate goodness in each of us, to the unity that is here, it creates room for the expansion for even more of the same. I truly believe that each one of us has the power to create balance in our world, to effect change based on ethical choices, to be better stewards of our home and all its inhabitants than ever before. The animals have given us a path to begin that journey. I'm excited to see how we shift our world to be more amazing than ever before.

The animals in this book have posed numerous questions and opened many doors to new conversations. We have opportunities to create deeper connections with them and with all life-forms, including humans. This book is not just about creating heart connections with nonhumans but also with ourselves and each other. They have given us tools to begin that journey, and it is my sincere hope that many of us will begin to walk that path of understanding, compassion, awareness, tolerance, and kindness for all.

There may be things that seem wildly out of balance in our world. I believe, though, that there is far more balance than there appears to be. What if this is more than just trying to fight the good fight or give up? The animals have shown me time and time again that we have access to higher realms, and there is a part of me that fears that. There are humans who I think would take it and harness it and use it for ill or to cause a collapse on this planet even sooner. But I cannot hold back my message based on the fear of what might happen. It's up to me to honor my path. It's up to me to share this, to tune in to these animals and share their message with anyone who is ready to listen. It's up to me to take their knowledge in the hopes that we can transform, that we can find unity, that we can find connection, that we can be more than we have been.

If any of these messages have pushed us out of our comfort zone or helped us to stop and be more aware—that's a good thing. What if everything they have told us is possible? What will we now do with this knowledge? Are we capable of understanding that animals are sentient beings and then still continue to cause them harm? How can we? When we get to the point that we see the birds and the mice and the chimpanzees as we would see our own family members, can we continue to cause them harm? Or will we take this as an opportunity to rise up and say no. No more cruel, unnecessary testing. No more animal fighting rings. No more inhumane slaughter processes. No more clubbing baby seals or killing wolf pups in order to make clothes that humans don't really need. No more killing of humans over differences that the ego can't handle.

Maybe this is our opportunity to stand up and show what a good, decent human looks like, that we are capable of making kind, compassionate choices—to each other, as well. Maybe it's also our opportunity to show that we understand the dynamics of supply and demand, and as long as we tell manufacturers what we are willing to give our money to, maybe they will have to change their ways, they will have to begin to eliminate animal testing or stop using plastic packaging and find ways to produce their products without causing harm. When we understand the gravity and the impact of our choices, we will also begin to protect this planet. It is time for humans to come together. It is time for humans to be more *humane* than we've ever been to the planet, to every living thing, and to each other. Yes, even each other. Every living being has a right to be here, a purpose for being here, and I believe that when we finally begin to accept each other exactly as we are, we will begin to shift the momentum of evolving into our higher selves. The animals have told us we are capable of it and that we are here to do just that while still alive. I believe we can, and I know the animals have given us tools to make it happen.

I still do struggle with some of these concepts the animals have shared in this book and all the questions they have posed, despite all the ways that they have opened my heart, especially those concepts that involve suffering, torture, and murder. There's a part of me that understands what they're saying and how in order for all that suffering and murder to cease to exist, it's up to us to acknowledge why it's there in the first place. I guess my fear, or my concern, is this: how do we shift from being where we currently are to being where we could be without all the suffering? My instinct tells me that it's up to each one of us to plant those seeds, to nurture those seeds, to help them grow and be strong - one step and one loving thought at a time.

It's also up to each one of us to look at the doors that the animals have opened for us and choose to walk through them. I believe what they have told us, I believe that we are not alone, and I have to believe that all of this is for a reason, that we are being pushed in order to create change. And it's a change that means all life-forms matter, that we all have a purpose, that we all have a right to live our lives, and that we can actually live those lives without fear, without suffering, without hatred. I have to believe that we can actually evolve into the kinds of human beings that the animals think that we can be. The messages they sent were clear, and they were also so unified in their belief of the connection and the unity of all life-forms. I choose to believe them, and I choose to believe that we, as humans, can evolve into our higher selves and deepen that connection with all life-forms.

The animals have asked us some tough questions, and the answers have many consequences. We are being given an opportunity to become kinder, more aware, more compassionate humans. One way we can do that is by acknowledging that we are not supreme beings here on Earth. We share this planet with other life-forms, many of them life-forms that we depend on for our survival. Is it in the realm of possibility that humans find balance and learn to truly coexist? Are we able to live a heart-centered life, understanding that we are all connected? I believe we are. I believe there are more of us who understand the balance of life, that have a grasp on the concept of the circle of life, and who are willing—maybe even eager—to live that life.

Taking steps to a more compassionate world is as easy as only purchasing items that are cruelty-free or only purchasing food from ranchers who have treated their animals humanely. We have incredible power as consumers, and we have such easy access now via social media to let manufacturers know that we only give our money to those who do not cause harm. We also do this by being open and accepting of the differences in each human. From what many of the animals have told us, the goal is not to all be alike but to honor our own paths, regardless of what those paths look like. I have to believe that we can live from our hearts, let go of the intolerance between us, and begin a new phase for humans that involves balance for each of us, tolerance for our differences, compassion for another's struggle, and a true desire for all humans to feel and connect on a deeper level.

I believe that each animal in this book has another

specific message for you—yes, you, the one reading this right now. My sincere hope is that you will revisit the pictures and be open to what they have to share with you. Listen with your heart and receive their messages with love. There are so many more animals waiting for us to hear their messages, too, and connect with them at a much deeper level. I am envisioning a future where humans live authentically from their hearts with meaning and compassion for all, and I can feel the animals celebrating this shift in each of us.

When I look back on what I thought were soul-crushing experiences in my life, I can see now that they also have been the most transformational experiences in my life. I wouldn't be where I am without them. Everything happens for a reason: Joey coming into my life, the heartbreak of his death leading me to Dr. Ryan, which led me to Reiki, which led me to a life full of love, healing, growth, evolution, and transformation. And now I'm passing that on to you in the hopes that you, too, will find your life filled with love, meaning, and connection to *all*.

SUGGESTED READING

- *Animals and Why They Matter* by Mary Midgley
- *A Practical Companion to Ethics* by Anthony Weston
- *Animals That Know When Their Owner is Coming Home* by Rupert Sheldrake
- *I L L U M I N A T I O N* by Jo Courtney
- *The True Power of Water* by Masaru Emoto (or anything by Masaru Emoto!)
- *Animal-Speak* by Ted Andrews
- *Are We Smart Enough to Know How Smart Animals Are?* by Frans de Waal
- *Beyond Words: What Animals Think and Feel* by Carl Safina

ABOUT SHAWNDRA

Shawndra has been communicating with animals since 2000. She is also an Usui and Karuna® Reiki Master, working with humans and animals. Shawndra is a past president of the Washington State Animal Response Team (WASART) and also serves on the board of directors with Kindred Souls Foundation, both 501c3 nonprofit organizations dedicated to helping animals. Shawndra began her disaster animal rescue work in 2005, after Hurricane Katrina made landfall, and she deployed outside of New Orleans, LA, to help rescue and care for the animals left behind. She has deployed to Chile, Peru, and to several states in the United States, volunteering to help animals recover from disasters. Shawndra also volunteered with Wolf Haven International in Tenino, WA, for nearly eight years and is still active in supporting their mission. She is the owner of Sanskrit Healing, using her skill to help humans, animals, and the environment find balance.